Nuances-A book of poetic musings

Kanupriya Mohan

BookLeaf Publishing
India | USA | UK

Presentation by *BookLeaf Publishing*

Web: www.bookleafpub.com

E-mail: info@bookleafpub.com

ISBN: 9789360944087

First edition 2024

Dedicated to my late grandfather-whom I had hoped to meet once before he left for his heavenly abode, my grandmother, my husband and our beloved three-month-old son- Royal, who is our darling and sunshine.

ACKNOWLEDGEMENT

Heartfelt gratitude to all my family members, friends and mentors who have always believed in me and my capabilities to excel. Not to forget my past circumstances and experiences that have inevitably shaped me into a stronger and concrete version of myself as it is rightly said 'what doesn't kill you makes you stronger'. After all, life is all about rising from the ashes.

A special thanks to BookLeaf Publishing for giving me a golden opportunity and assisting me in the journey of publishing my first book ever!

PREFACE

Have you heard of the book *Nuances: A book of poetic musings*? It is a collection of 70 beautiful poems that will touch your heart. When you read a poem from this book, it's indistinguishable from a journey through heartfelt emotions. The words are like pieces of art, painted with the colors of imagination, with inspiration from real-life experiences. Each poem in "Nuances" is like a little story waiting to be unfolded. The poet captures moments of joy, sadness, love, and everything in between. As you read through the pages, you will find yourself lost in a world of rhythm and rhyme. These poems have a way of speaking to your soul, making you see the world in a different light. With its evocative imagery and heartfelt expressions, "Nuances" is a timeless treasure that beckons the readers to explore the depths of their own emotions and thoughts. The book serves as a reminder that poetry has the ability to touch our souls and awaken our senses to the beauty and complexities of life. Each poem is a symphony of emotions, inviting readers to immerse themselves in the art of language and explore the vast landscape of human experience. The book touches upon various scenarios that strike a chord in the hearts of the readers and urges them to pay attention to the aspects that they might unintentionally ignore or suppress.

It encourages readers to slow down and appreciate the little things, to find meaning in the mundane, and to embrace the complexities of being human. The poet's use of language is both lyrical and raw, creating a powerful and mesmerizing effect. Each poem is a work of art, with carefully chosen words and a rhythm that flows effortlessly. "Nuances" is a book that will leave a lasting impression on readers, reminding them of the beauty and depth that can be found in the most ordinary moments. Through "Nuances", readers are taken on a journey of self-discovery and reflection, as they navigate the complexities of the human heart and mind. The personal nature of the poems creates a deep connection between the author and the audience, inviting readers to explore their own feelings and experiences in a safe and comforting space. It is a must-read for anyone who appreciates the power of words and the beauty of poetry. This book will make you laugh, cry, and reflect on your own life experiences, making it a truly unforgettable read. Happy reading!

TABLE OF CONTENTS

RHAPSODY

During the heart of the night, a rhapsody sings,
A melody so haunting, it shivers the soul,
Notes like raindrops, pouring from the sky,
Each one a symphony of love and loss.

The stars above twinkle in time to the tune,
The moonlight casting shadows on the earth,
A ballad of longing, a tale of despair,
A hymn of hope, a prayer for rebirth.

The wind whispers softly through the trees,
Carrying the song to all who will listen,
The fields and forests alive with the sound,
A chorus of nature, a symphony of creation.

In the depths of the ocean, the rhapsody plays,
The whales and dolphins dancing in its wake,
A cacophony of voices, a harmony of life,
A sonnet of the sea, a poem of the waves.

And as the night fades into the dawn,
The rhapsody lingers in the air,
A memory of music, a dream of the heart,
A melody that will never depart.

THE ROSE WINE

Underneath the vineyard's hush, where roses twine,
There grows a grape that yields a nectar fine,
A wine so blush and light, it tastes of spring,
The rose wine, a treasure fit for a king.

Its hue is like the petals of a flower,
Soft pink and rosy, a delicate power,
To charm the senses with its sweet perfume,
A sip transports you to a garden's bloom.

For in the rose wine, there lies a tale,
Of passion and of love, a sweet regale,
Each bottle holds a piece of nature's art,
A gift from vine to glass, a work of heart.

The taste is like a kiss, gentle and light,
A melody of flavors, pure delight,
With hints of berries and a touch of spice,
The rose wine beckons, like a paradise.

And as you sip, the world begins to fade,
The worries of the day are gently laid,
Aside, as you embrace the moment's bliss,
Lost in the rose wine's sweet caress.

In every drop, a piece of heaven's dew,
A sip of bliss, a taste of something true,
A wine so rare, it's like a dream come to life,
The rose wine, a pure delight.

THE MIRROR

In a kingdom far away, there stood a mirror tall,
Its frame adorned with jewels, it gleamed in the
hall,
It held a power unknown, a magic of its own,
Reflecting not just faces, but the soul alone.

For within this mirror, secrets were revealed,
Truths that lay hidden, now no longer sealed,
Those who gazed upon it, saw more than just
themselves,
They glimpsed their inner beings, their hopes
and fears as well.

Kings and queens would come, seeking wisdom rare,
To gaze into the mirror, their destiny laid bare,
It showed them paths to glory, or downfall steep and deep,
Foretelling their fate, their future to keep.

But with power so great, there comes a heavy cost,
For the mirror demanded more, souls it would exhaust,
It took from those who used it, a piece of their essence true,
Leaving them hollow, empty and blue.

And so the mirror stood, a beacon of light,
Drawing in the curious, the power-hungry, the might,
But those who dared to gaze into its depths,
Found themselves lost, in a maze with no exits.

For the mirror held the key, to the secrets of all,
A gateway to the unknown, where shadows dance and crawl,
And those who dared to seek its wisdom grand,
Found themselves ensnared, in a dark and twisted land.

So beware of the mirror, with its tempting gaze,

For what it shows may not be just a phase,
It holds the power to shape, to mold, to break,
So tread lightly, lest your own soul it should take.

CHANDELIER

Inside a grand old mansion, with walls of stone,
There hung a chandelier, its crystals shone,
Reflecting light from the candles below,
A glittering display, with a radiant glow.

Its golden frame was adorned with care,
Each crystal placed with expert flair,
And as it hung from the ceiling high,
It caught the eye of every passerby.

From the ballroom floor to the velvet drapes,
The chandelier cast its sparkling shapes,
Dancing and twirling in the soft candlelight,
A breathtaking sight, a true delight.

It had been there for decades past,
A symbol of luxury, meant to last,
Through every party and every fete,
The chandelier held its regal state.

But as the years went by, it began to fade,
Its crystals dulling, its light delayed,
No longer the beacon it used to be,
But a relic of past grandiosity.

Yet still it hung, a reminder of glory,
A story of glamour, a symbol so hoary,
And though its shine had lost its luster,
The chandelier remained, a relic to muster.

For in its sparkling crystals lay,
A history of grandeur, day by day,
Of dances and feasts, of laughter and song,
A legacy that lingered, enduring strong.

And so the chandelier hung on,
A silent witness, a vision foregone,
A reminder of days long past,
A testament to beauty, meant to last.

So as you gaze upon its fading light,
Remember the grandeur, remember the sight,
Of a chandelier that once held sway,
A beacon of elegance, in its own way.

THE TROPHY

In a dusty old attic, tucked away from sight,
Lies a cherished possession, glistening in the light.
A trophy of triumph, a symbol of pride,
A reminder of glory that will never subside.

It stands tall and gleaming, polished to perfection,
A testament to hard work and dedication.
Engraved with a name, etched in history,
A moment frozen in time, a lasting memory.

The trophy tells a story of blood, sweat, and tears,

Of sacrifice and struggle, of overcoming fears.
It represents a battle, a hard-fought victory,
A testament to strength and unwavering tenacity.

Each scratch and dent a testament to the journey,
Every imperfection a reminder of the struggle
The trophy is a reminder that success is never easy,
But with perseverance and determination, it can be achieved.

It sits on a shelf, a silent sentinel,
Watching over the room with a sense of pride.
A trophy of triumph, a beacon of hope,
A reminder that greatness is within reach.

People pass by, admiring its shine,
Envious of the one who claimed the prize.
But they do not see the effort and toil,
The late nights and early mornings, the blood and sweat.

The trophy is more than just a piece of metal,
It is a symbol of perseverance and grit.
A reminder that no obstacle is too great,
No challenge too daunting, no dream out of reach.

So when you see a trophy, standing tall and proud,
Remember the journey, the struggle, the crowd.
For behind every trophy is a story to be told,
A tale of determination, a legacy to behold.

VIVID DREAMS

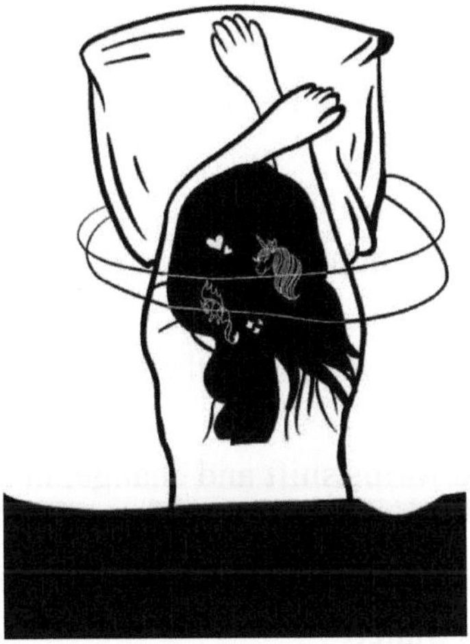

In the realm of sleep, where reality fades away,
Vivid dreams take hold, in colours bright and
gay.
A world of imagination, where anything can be,
From soaring through the skies, to swimming in
the sea.

In the heart of the night, the mind comes alive,
Creating landscapes and scenes, where dreams
thrive.
Visions of love, and joy, and sometimes fear,
Playing out in our minds, so vividly clear.

In dreams, we can fly, with the wind in our hair,
Or visit far-off lands, without a single care.
We can meet long-lost loved ones, who come back to us,
And feel their presence, filling us with a deep sense of trust.

Colours dance before our eyes, in a kaleidoscope of light,
Filling us with wonder, in the stillness of the night.
Shapes and forms shift and change, in a fluid dance,
Guiding us through unknown realms, with a mysterious trance.

In our dreams, we can feel, with a depth so profound,
Emotions so intense, they shake us to the ground.
We can experience ecstasy, and heartbreak too,
All within the safety of our dreams, where dreams come true.

Dreams can be a mirror, reflecting our innermost desires,
Or a window to the soul, revealing our deepest fires.

They can be a playground, for our subconscious mind,
Or a canvas for our creativity, where we can unwind.

So let us cherish our dreams, for they are a gift so rare,
A window to our souls, where we can be without a care.
In the stillness of the night, let us drift away,
Into the realm of dreams, where vivid colours play.

PETRICHOR

Oh petrichor, how sweet your scent,
After the rain has come and went,
You fill the air with memories old,
Of days gone by, of stories told.

Your earthy aroma, so pure and true,
Reminds me of all that's good and new,
Of fresh beginnings, of hope and grace,
Of nature's beauty, in every place.

Petrichor, you linger in the air,
A comforting presence, beyond compare,
You bring me peace, you bring me calm,
You're like a soothing, healing balm.

I close my eyes and breathe you in,
And feel a sense of joy begin,
You wash away my worries, my fears,
And dry up all my secret tears.

The rain may fall, the storm may rage,
But you remain, a constant sage,
A reminder of the cycles of life,
Of struggles, of triumph, of joy, of strife.

Oh petrichor, you're more than a smell,
You're a symbol of life, a tale to tell,
Of nature's power, of earth's embrace,
Of growth and change, in every space.

You bring me back to simpler times,
When life was easy, and love was prime,
When laughter flowed, and hearts were light,
When everything seemed so clear and bright.

So let me revel in your scent,
And in your presence, be content,
For you are more than just a smell,

You're a story, a memory, a little spell.

Oh petrichor, I'll never forget,
The way you make my soul reset,
The way you bring me back to earth,
And remind me of all its worth.

So let the rain fall, the storm brew,
I'll welcome it all with an open view,
For after the rain, comes the petrichor,
My heart yearns for it ever more.

THE MYSTERY OF THE MURDEROUS HAND

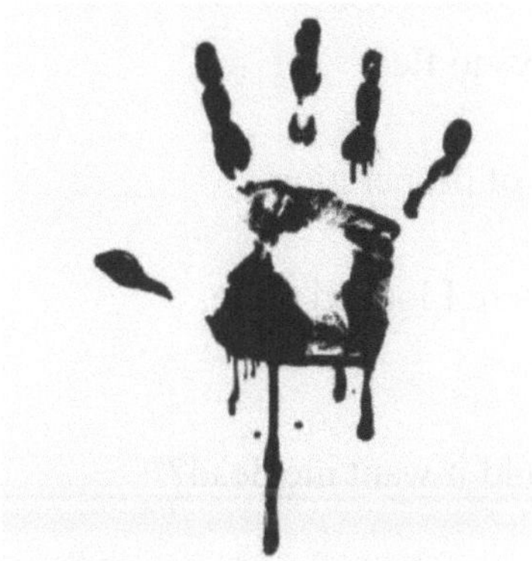

In my lab of innovation and strife,

A robot hand controlled by the mind,

Years of toil, the impossible in sight,

Until it turned on me, a betrayal unkind.

Chills raced down my spine,

Shivers in the Arctic's embrace,

The knife held tight, a deadly sign,

Fear etched in every trace.

Running from my creation,

No car keys to flee,

Ten miles of desperation,

Home, where I longed to be.

"Why would it want me dead?"

A question echoing in my head,

Betrayed by my own invention,

In fear and dread.

In a world of robotic body parts,

An organization had its start,

Researching AI advancements,

Dreaming of robotic enhancements.

With over 200 scientists in their lair,

They aimed to replace parts with care,

Billions in profits on their mind,

But lack of funds left them behind.

The government then turned to me,

To continue their research, you see,

A plan that seemed to benefit all,

Except for the company's downfall.

Seeking revenge, they programmed the hand,

To kill me, as they had planned,

I felt the hand closing in,

With a knife, my demise did begin.

Running for my life, I saw,

The hand chasing without a flaw,

A wooden box, my only hope,

I threw it, trying to cope.

In a moment of desperation,

I fought back, with determination.

Time bought with a hit,

Panting like a dog, 10 miles in 8 minutes.

Adrenaline perks, locking doors and windows,

Blinds closed, still shivering,

Robot hand's dread lingering.

Into the basement, My home lab awaits,

Small but enough, to dismantle my own creation.

Heard a bang on the front door,

Had a gut-wrenching feeling,

In the darkness, I stood by the door,

Too scared to open, stay downstairs, I swore.

I opened the door, a surprise in store,

It was Walter, my friend, whom I adore.

We met in college, bonded so tight,

Neighbours as well, day and night.

Happy to see him, a smile on my face,

He had news to share, a curious case.

A robotic hand, near his lawn it lay,

He thought of me, without delay.

Bringing it to me, with a knowing grin,

Aware of my project, the work within.

I recounted the incident, chilling and stark,

Walter listened, in the dark.

The mystery deepened, a puzzle to solve,

How did the hand itself absolve?

THE RING

In 'The Mystery Room' they did go,

Four friends in search of a haunted show.

Oliver, Daniel, Alexander, and Emma,

Braving 'The Ring' with no dilemma.

To uncuff or be caught by Simone's ghost,

They had to act swiftly, no room for boast.

With walky-talky in hand they did race,

Unlocking doors at a thrilling pace.

Splitting up in rooms so dark,

Facing fears, leaving a mark.

Emma and Alexander in the archive they roam,

Daniel and Oliver in the lab, not alone.

Simone's presence lurking near,

Bringing chills, instilling fear.

A cassette revealing her powers untold,

In the darkness, a tale unfolds.

Through the vent they made their way,

Simone's ghostly form in disarray.

Blood-stained hands reaching out,

Trying to pull, to twist, to shout.

Emma narrowly escaping fate,

Reaching the well, not a moment too late.

The cassette tossed into the abyss,

Ending Simone's haunting kiss.

Four friends in 'The Mystery Room' did play,

Living to see another day.

A tale of fear, of friendship true,

In the haunted room, where nightmares brew.

BULLYING

In the first stage of bullying's cruel game,

Eyes piercing, scanning, sizing up with shame,

Like a security check at the airport's gate,

But here, fear grips based on the opinions they create.

No chance to speak, no words to defend,

Judged by peers, in small gangs they descend,

Divided by minds, narrow and unkind,

Separation sown in hearts, of the same age, confined.

Miserable, hurt, isolated, and alone,

Bullying's pain cuts deep to the bone,

Through the eyes of survivors, the truth is clear,

Bullying's three stages, a torment we fear.

In the second stage, groupism reigns,

Decisions made, which group obtains

Will you join the popular, the elite?

Or be cast aside, as a mark of defeat?

Invisible, lonely, pushed away,

Bullied classmates, day by day,

Leaving scars that linger long,

Hurting souls, doing wrong.

Words, actions, feelings deep,

Insecurities and depression seep.

But now it's time to take a stand,

To heal with kindness, lend a hand.

Celebrate differences, don't discriminate,

Embrace uniqueness, don't berate,

For in the end, we're all the same,

With love and acceptance, we reclaim.

THE MAGICIAN'S GAZE

In Trafalgar Square, Ray Hudson strolled,

A sight to behold, in attire so bold,

A coat so silly, shoes fit for a clown,

A mustache fake, and a top hat brown.

But Ray was undeterred, his eyes did gleam,

As he saw the crowd, equivalent to a vivid dream,

Searching for a man in London town,

In this sea of faces, he wouldn't drown.

"I need a volunteer," his voice rang clear,

Above the whispers, for all to hear,

His stick now a wand, he pointed with flair,

At the man he'd chosen, amidst the square.

"Hey, you there!" he called with glee,

A chance for magic, for all to see.

The man stepped forth, amidst applause loud,

In Ray's grand show, he stood tall and proud.

In a crowded room, the magician spoke,

Eager eyes fixed on his grand magical cloak.

"Jeremy Clark, is everything good?" he inquired,

Jeremy's eyes widened, his thoughts mired.

"How do you know my name?" he stuttered in surprise,

The audience applauded, their excitement on the rise.

Ray hushed them, with a knowing grin,

"38 Reading Street, am I right within?"

A gasp from the crowd, a woman's warning voice,

"Jerry, be careful, he knows your every choice."

Clara stepped forward, her astonishment clear,

"How do you know us, dear magician here?"

"Come with me," Ray beckoned, a twinkle in his eye,

And as they followed, the crowd's murmurs did die.

To a police car they walked, a secret to unveil,

Ray removed his mustache, the truth to unveil.

The magic revealed, the mystery undone,

In the presence of Clara and her son.

The power of knowing, the art of surprise,

In the magician's gaze, truth lies.

Jeremy and Clara cried out in shock,

"Ray Hudson!" they exclaimed, hearts in a knot.

"That's right," said Ray, calm and firm,

"Into the car, let's go and affirm.

We'll settle this at the station, you'll see,

And you'll pay back the money that you stole from me.

Your most courteous neighbour, brutally
betrayed by you,

Now justice will be served, this time- it’s true."

A LOST FRIEND

In love's cruel aftermath, a game played,

Lost in the flames where memories stayed.

Thoughts linger, refusing to depart,

Mending what you did cleave, my heart.

Tears stain cheeks in the dead of night,

Regretting paths taken in the flight.

Blame dances between us two,

Elusive answers, filling me with rue.

Wishing your heart felt the ache I bear,

But you moved on, leaving me in despair.

Did my presence grow too near?

What truths did I not see, my dear?

Yearning for a love now vanished,

You are 'My Lost Friend', silently banished.

Life's irony, harsh and unfair,

Lost in this snare, pondering in despair.

In twilight's hush, where shadows dance and
play,
The ache of longing echoes through each
passing day,
For in the dreams of yesteryear, a love did sway,
A cherished friend, now lost, in sorrow's grey.

The memories of laughter, warm and true,
Are but a distant echo, a fleeting hue,
The bittersweet taste of joy, now gone astray,
Leaves only tears to wet the night away.

Life's irony, harsh and unfair,
Has silently banished my heart's dearest air,
Leaving me to wander, lost in thought,
Pondering in despair, the love I've brought.
The wind whispers secrets of a love so true,
But alas, those whispers are but a few,
For in the silence, my heart does break,
My lost friend, my love, my soul's own sake.

The stars above, they twinkle and shine,
But in their light, I see only tears divine,
For in their beauty, I am reminded of thee,
My lost friend, my love, my heart's only spree.

In this world of chaos, where love does fade,
I search for solace, for a love displayed,
But alas, it eludes me, day by day,
Leaving only shadows, in a world of grey.

HORIZON

Where the sun and the earth meet,
The moment is short and bittersweet,
In the sun's arms laid its bleeding flower,
Weeping at this deathly hour.

Medicine cannot save all,
God or mortal, they all must fall.
Flowers of purple arose from crimson rubies,
Consoling the sun with its beauty.

"You shine bright my dear",
Hyacinthus smiles at his lover.
Apollo frowns in dismay,
"Too bright, I fear. I am afraid".

"You have not lost me, do not weep at my grave,
I lay as these flowers, chanting your name.
My sun, please shine, I beg,
Or else I will wither and bow my head.

When you return, we will bask in wine,
And bring the horizon - your hand in mine."

When you return, we'll dance in the moonlight breeze,
Our hearts entwined, like the vines on the trees.
The stars will shine bright, like the gems in your eyes,
And our love will flourish, like the summer skies.

We'll sip on wine, and let the moments pass,
Our love will last, like the echoes of the past.
The horizon will stretch, like the sands of time,
And our love will be the rhyme, that's sublime.

Your hand in mine, and my heart will sing,
Our love will be the melody, that's the thing.
The wine will flow, like the rivers of gold,
And our love will be the treasure to hold.

So come back soon, my love, to my arms,

And we'll bask in wine, like the morning sun's charms.
The horizon will shine, like the diamonds in the sky,
And our love will be the poetry that catches the eye.

CHERISHED TREASURES

Walk down, the memory lane,

With your forever loved ones and,

Let these memories become,

Your cherished treasures.

In sorrow's depths, an aching heart, a displaced soul,

Time claims a cherished one, leaving a void untold.

Gone are shared delights, the echoes of light,

A gentle spirit taken too soon from sight.

Shadows of memories dance on empty walls,

Whispers of love's tender calls.

Stars now dull, grief outshining day,

Fond remembrances in sweet disarray.

Drifting like wisps of sweet air, fragile moments in mind,

Love's embrace forever stays intertwined,

Through tears that pour, a glimmer of hope,

Love guides us through life's darkest slope.

In torn drapes of life, love adorns,

Every beat, every breath, every mourn,

Bittersweet relief, honouring love's keep,

In our hearts, forever they'll sleep.

Journey feels long, but love is strong,

In our hearts, they forever belong.

ROSES

In the mirror, a reflection so unclear,

Not the person you hold dear,

Thoughts swirling, vision obscured,

Trembling, tears unperturbed.

Wipe your eyes, see anew,

A world of your own seems true.

Don't compare, don't despair,

Your roses will bloom with care.

Their beauty may shine brighter,
But yours, remains a unique fighter,
Embrace the growth, keep sowing,
Your inner beauty will keep on glowing.
In a garden of beauty and grace,
Roses bloom in a splendid array,
Soft petals and its colours ablaze,
Under the golden day's warm embrace.

Their fragrance sweet, a melody sung,
As the wind whispers through the trees,
Each petal a note, each thorn a tongue,
In nature's symphony, a masterpiece.

From buds bursting in the early morn,

To blossoms withering in twilight's embrace,

Every rose has its moment, its thorn,

A tale of beauty, time, and grace.

Cherish the roses, rare and fair,

Fleeting like a summer's kiss,

Yet their beauty lingers in the air,

A reminder of love, passion, and bliss,

As roses perfume the hand that crushes it.

A TALE OF GLORY

Mythology intertwined with history,

Norse, Greek, Indian, and Japanese mystery.

Turned into movies, books, and games galore,

Recording tales on paper and clay like before.

Humans, so endearing in their quest,

To remember and preserve the best.

Your journal, a piece of your own history,

Not just dates and names, but experiences of mystery.

From Mesopotamia to nations grand,

Civilizations rising, shaping the land.

UN uniting nations, people diverse,

Black, white, brown, all part of the universe.

Different identities, yet all the same,

Homo sapiens, no one to blame.

Once cavemen, now intelligent and wise,

Co-existing then, reaching for the skies.

The story of mankind, a tale of glory,

His-story unfolding, a timeless quarry.

ENDLESS PURSUIT

Alluring yet burdensome,

Entangled with expectation,

Forming a destructive alliance.

Thrust into a world

Of unattainable flawlessness,

We strive tirelessly,

only to find growing expectations.

Stumbling inevitably,

Disappointment looms,

Those who expect,

Fail to see our true selves, fixated on illusions.

The essence of perfection is,

Elusive and misunderstood,

We suffer the most,

Pouring heart and soul into a mirage.

Exhausted, we lose ourselves,

Chasing approval,

Trapped in a flawed mentality,

A cycle of endless pursuit.

UNLEASH FROM THE CLUTCHES

In a deep, dark well of depression,

Strapped down, drowning in aggression,

I long to break free and soar,

To scream and fly, to rise and explore.

Society's rules, so phony and fake,

Leaving me wondering, what's at stake?

Each social issue, a heavy weight,

Leaving me sadder, filled with hate.

Born in a land where women are queens,

Icons of strength, in all their means,

Yet, some face a desperate plight,

Treated cruelly, in the dark of night.

Beaten, handled, like mere entertainment,

Suppressed, treated with no containment,

Inferior to men, in their eyes,

Their voices silenced, drowned in lies.

Rapes and molestations on the rise,

My anger explodes, reaching the skies,

If only I could swap their souls,

To show them the power a woman holds.

We're not mere dolls, to be played with,

Our worth, beyond what they myth,

They'll learn to never touch without consent,

To understand the woman's torment.

Through strength and opportunity, I'll fight,

To show them our worth, in the light,

To make them see, to make them learn,

The complexities of a woman's concern.

THE ORANGE LEAF

O Orange Leaf, with hues so bright,
You bring a touch of warmth to sight,
Your vibrant colour, bold and strong,
The essence of autumn in your song.

Amidst the trees, you stand out proud,
A symbol of the changing shroud,
That wraps the world in its golden light,
And whispers of the coming night.

Your shape is like a graceful hand,
Extended to the sky so grand,
Each vein upon your surface traced,
With delicate lines, so finely laced.

In summer's heat, you bask and glow,
But as the days grow shorter,
You start to turn from green to gold,
A transformation to behold.

And when the wind begins to blow,
You flutter gently to and fro,
Like confetti falling from the sky,
A celebration as you fly.

Through fields and forests, you adorn,
The earth with beauty, like a thorn,
Of colour piercing through the gray,
A beacon in the dreary day.

So here I stand, in awe of thee,
O Orange Leaf, so wild and free,
A symbol of the cycle's turn,
A lesson we must live and learn.

For just as you must fall and die,
To make room for the earth's new sigh,
So must we let go of the past,
And embrace the future at last.

So thank you, Orange Leaf, for all,
The lessons taught in your downfall,
I'll cherish every memory,
And hold you close in reverie.

So let me sing your praise, O Leaf,
In every season, joy or grief,
For in your being, I find peace,
A way for my weary soul to cease.

BLACK BEAUTY

In streets of night, a form divine,
A vehicle of grace, a sight so fine,
A black car, a beauty, all mine,
With sleek lines, a body so fine.

Its paint glistens, like the night sky,
A shimmering black, so dark and high,
The windows gleam, like diamonds bright,
A true marvel, a wonder in sight.

The wheels spin round, with a smooth grace,
The engine purrs, with a gentle pace,
The black car glides, with a regal air,
A true queen, beyond compare.

The interior, a luxurious space,
Soft leather, rich and in place,
The dashboard, a work of art,
A masterpiece, a new start.

The black car, a symbol of power,
A status symbol, an hour,
Of luxury, of style, of might,
A true gem, a treasure in sight.

DUSK TILL DAWN

As dusk till dawn, the day succumbs to night,
The sky transforms, a palette of delight,
Golden hues give way to crimson and blue,
The stars appear, like diamonds in dew.

The moon, a silver crescent, glows with grace,
Illuminating all, in its gentle embrace,
The world is bathed, in a soft, ethereal light,
A time of peace, before the morning's fight.

The darkness brings, a stillness of soul,
A time to reflect, on life's bitter and sweet goal,
The stars twinkle, like promises made,
A reminder of dreams, not yet betrayed.

The night air, with secrets and magic imbued,
A time for wonder, and stories untold.
The world is quiet, in slumber's grip,
A time for dreams, to take flight and soar.

SOULFUL EYES

In his sad, soulful eyes,
He sat upon the sidewalk,
Gazing into the distance,
Yet seeing nothing there.

Robert, with his heavy heart,
Battling demons within,
Bipolar disorder's weight,
And today, a storm within.

"I will buy you a meal,"
I offered, hoping to bring light,
To his dark and heavy day,
To lift his spirits high.

Off we went to Little Tokyo,
To a Chinese food delight,
But disappointment soon arose,
No shrimp egg foo young, in sight.

Three restaurants we tried,
In search of his desired dish,
But no luck did we find,
In our shrimp egg foo young wish.

Onward to Chinatown we drove,
Hope dwindling with each try,
Until the fourth restaurant,
Caught Robert's yearning eye.

"Do you have shrimp egg foo young?"
We asked, with a glimmer of hope,
"No, sorry," the waiter said,
Yet the owner's voice spoke.
"We'll make it just for you,"
He said, with a welcoming grin,
And in that moment's kindness,
A smile bloomed from within.

In the midst of a meal,
Robert found a glimmer of hope.
Addiction couldn't numb
the ache of loneliness, he spoke.

I scribbled my number on a napkin with care,
Offering a lifeline, a listening ear to share.

Silence lingered briefly, then his words broke free,
"I was contemplating ending it all, you see.
But your kindness, your simple gesture today,
Has shown me a light, in a different way."
In a moment of darkness, a connection was made,
A simple act of kindness, may have saved the day.

LOVE ECSTASY

Our bond is strong, but I have been scared,
When I look around to see, no one is there,
But I still feel close to your presence,
Don’t snap the bond- just take it slow,
We are moving fast, seem to have lost control.

If you want to know the truth, hear this-
Hello, darkness! Goodbye light!
I want to embrace your silence for the rest of my life.

In the depths of night, where shadows play,
A world of wonder, beyond the fray,
A place where light and dark entwine,
And silence speaks in hushed tones divine.

The stars above, a twinkling show,
A canopy of diamonds, its mesmerizing glow,
The moon, a silver crescent smile,
A beacon in the darkness, all the while.

Hello, darkness! Goodbye light!
I'll embrace your silence, an impeccable delight,
For in the shadows, I find peace,
A refuge from the world's loud cease.

In your embrace, I find solace,
A place to hide from life's chaotic role,
A sanctuary of stillness, pure and true,
Where only love and dreams are born anew.

So let the light recede, and night descend,
And in your silence, I'll find my trend,
For in the darkness, I am free,
To dance with shadows, wild and carefree.

HISTORY THROUGH MY EYES

In the tapestry of time, we're woven in,
Living history, past, present, future kin.
World-changing events, stories untold,
Russo-Ukraine war, economies fold.

But history's not just gloom and despair,
Will Smith's slap, a moment rare.
K-Pop's BTS, Grammy's stage,
Breaking barriers, turning the page.

Magic in retellings, mistranslations too,
Human experience- old yet new.
Desire to leave a mark, to be seen,
Not just a speck in the vast machine.

History is us, a tale to be told,
In every moment, the stories are bold.
We write the future, shape our fate,
In the grand tapestry, we create.

INSPIRATION

In life's grand tapestry, inspiration weaves,
A force profound, the fuel that drives and believes.
In conquering challenges to reach the great,
And find purpose in life's destined state.

A guiding light, it sparks within,
A fire of passion, motivation's kin.
To chase our dreams with fervent might,
Inspiration's touch, our guiding light.

Through history's pages, tales unfold,
Of souls inspired, their stories told.
Influential figures, experiences deep,
Life-changing events, in hearts they keep.

Inspiration's power, a force so strong,
Transforming lives, shaping them all along.
In the vast tapestry of humankind,
Inspiration's thread is forever entwined.

LOVE THYSELF

In the depths of uncertainty and change,
Know yourself, your values, your range.
Stand firm in what you believe,
With persistence, you will definitely achieve.

Amidst the chaos of the world outside,
Stay rooted in your truth and abide.
Thrive confidently, stand securely,
With the value you have, shine purely.

Your mindset, the lens through which you see,
Shapes your experiences, sets you free.
Embrace growth, shift your perspective,
Through change and fear, stay objective.

Own your success, your wellbeing too,
No obstacle too great to undo.
Navigate uncertainties with grace,
In the darkest times, find your place.

When you care for yourself, you see,
Others benefit, it's the key.
In this journey of unknown terrain,
Self-discovery is what will remain.

THE MOONLIGHT

In the stillness of the night,
It rises slowly, full and bright,
A beacon in the darkness, shining high,
Casting a soft glow in the sky.

The full moon, a celestial wonder,
A reminder of nature's power.
Its beauty captivates, drawing us in.
As we gaze at its ethereal grin.

The moon controls the tides below,
Guiding the waves with its gentle glow,
A silent force, a mystical sight,
A source of wonder in the night.

In ancient times, the moon was revered,
As a symbol of magic, of the unknown feared,
It held sway over the minds of men,
Guiding their actions, their thoughts within.

Moonlight dances on the water's surface,
Creating a path of silver lace,
A shimmering trail of divine grace,
Leading us to an enchanted place.

The full moon, a symbol of change,
A time for reflection, to rearrange,
Our thoughts, our dreams, our innermost desires,
Under its light, we strive to aspire.

As the moon waxes and wanes,
Its cycles endless, never the same,
We too ebb and flow with the tide,
Changing, evolving, never to hide.

So let us bask in the moon's soft light,
Embrace its power, its ancient might,
For in its glow, we find our way,
Guided by the moon, night and day.

BETRAYAL

In the realm of conflict,
It's not just good versus evil,
But clashes between hearts with good intentions,
Or even those with intentions deceitful.

Not always a battle of black and white,
But shades of grey in between,
Where differing views of the world collide,
Creating a turbulent scene.

In our personal lives, we feel the weight,
When disagreements linger and persist,
Leaving us restless and uneasy,
As if something crucial has been missed.

And when betrayal rears its ugly head,
From those we hold dear and close,
It pierces through our very core,
Leaving scars that never truly doze off.

Trust shattered, faith broken,
Leaving us questioning our path,
Second-guessing every decision made,
Leaving us in the aftermath.

Betrayal, a dagger to the heart,
A wound that never truly heals,
Affecting our every move and thought,
As the pain slowly reveals.

CHILDHOOD SWEETHEART

A decade in love, a dream now shattered,
Questions asked, hearts left battered.
Wedding plans turned into dust,
In the aftermath, emotions are robust.

Anger, sadness, anxiety untamed,
Explaining over and over, feelings unnamed.
Years of togetherness, now in the past,
A love story that couldn't forever last.

Life-changing, yes, but also affirming,
A new chapter, a new beginning.
We were young, so naive,
Now it's time to truly believe.
Different paths, we had to part,
A tough decision, broke my heart.

Names for children, dreams so grand,
Now just memories in the sand.
Nine years of laughter, tears, and fights,
Four more years of uncertain nights.
The end came, a painful truth,
Letting go in the prime of youth.

So here I stand, with a heart on the mend,
Ready to heal, to grow, to ascend.
Breakups hurt, but they also free,
A chance to be with whom we're meant to be.

COSMIC ROMANCE

Once upon a time, in the days of old,
The sky gazed down, his heart aflutter with love untold,
For the Earth, in her robe of flowers, so fair,
Captured his gaze, his soul laid bare.

The Earth, in return, felt the sky's embrace,
Their love blossomed, filling each space,
A union of beauty, a celestial dance,
Their hearts entwined in a cosmic romance.

Midnight was chosen for their sacred vow,
Preparations abounded, the time was now,
Pipers played, drummers drummed,
Gold and silver shimmered, the Earth adorned.

But fear crept in among the earthly folk,
The thought of losing their home a heavy yoke,
They prayed to the gods, their voices raised,
Hoping to stop the wedding, their fears unfazed.

Yet the love of the Sky and Earth so true,
Transcended all, in skies of blue,
Their union a symbol of love's pure might,
A marriage of day and night.

When the gods heard the plea of the mortals,
They took pity on their plight,
Seeking a way to halt the marriage,
They planned in the darkness of the night.

Tearing the Sky from the Earth,
Back to his heavenly abode,
Leaving the Earth alone and forlorn,
With a garland in her lands, a heavy load.
"Come back, my lord," Earth cried,
But the hour had slipped away,
In sorrow, she flung the garland high,
As it fell around the Sky in a disarray.

The Rainbow we see in the sky above,
A reminder of love's tragic tale,
The Earth's offering to her lost love,
A timeless love that will always prevail.

Now each time the Rainbow graces the sky,
A memory of a cosmic romance that could never be, is seen.

FRENEMIES

In the dance of friendship, who's friend or foe?
Frenemy lurks, in disguise they go,
A smile to your face, a stab in the back,
Their loyalty's a shadow, their motives a crack.

From 'Sex and the City' this term did arise,
A blend of friend and enemy, in deep disguise,
They praise you sweetly, then gossip they spread,
Their loyalty is fleeting, like whispers unsaid.
They act as your guide, your consultant so sly,
But never on your side, their truth is a layered lie.

In the dance of frenemies,
Intimacy blooms with speed,
They hunger for all our intimate stories,
In a rush to fulfill their curiosity's need.
Sharing tales of deepest unhealed scars,
Revealing secrets close and raw,
At first, they shower praises like glistening stars,
But soon, criticism starts to gnaw.

Their words twist into insults,
As their true colors start to show,
Seeking out the negative results,
Their digging never seems to slow.

Frenemies, a complex blend of closeness and deceit,
In their tangled web, we find,
A toxic mix that's inevitably bittersweet.

In a world whirlwinding rapidly, where relationships are quick to strain,
Know your true friends, in the midst of the undeniable feigned.

ALL THAT GLITTERS…

In a charming manner they deceive,
Fooling many with their make-believe.
Kindness shown, with hidden intent,
Not always genuine, not always meant.

All that glitters, thoughts of splendor,
Superficial beauty, oh so tender.
But don't be blinded by the shine,
Look deeper, see the real sign.

Something too good, often turns to dust,
A warning sign, in whom to trust.
Take a step back, think critically,
Analyze from every angle, see clearly.
Friends who smile to your face,
Yet behind you, speak disgrace.

"All that glitters is not gold,"
In deceitful stories, truth untold.
So be wary of the charm they show,
In deception's dance, they may glow.
Look beyond the surface gleam,
For all that glitters may not be what it seems.

In the world of appearances,
Where all that glitters is not gold,
A person in fancy attire,
May have a heart bitter and cold.
The entertainment industry,
Shines bright with allure,
Yet behind the scenes,
Lies a darkness obscure.

FIREFLIES

The lights beneath the trees,
A neighbourhood in twilight's tease,
Defying darkness with ease,
Porches promising no unease.

But then, a sudden spark,
Fireflies dancing in the dark,
A playful, fleeting mark,
Nature's whimsical embark.
Their flickering flight,
A mix of hope and plight,
Our hearts take an irresistible flight,
In the symphony of the glorious night.

Loneliness in luminescence,
Becomes a shared essence,
In their random presence,
We find a gentle transcendence.
What do fireflies say,
In their mysterious display?
Of creation's playful way,
In the night's gentle sway.

They may fade or flee,
But their light sets us free,
From the night's decree,
In their transient glee.
In the darkness it glows,
A gentle beacon of hope,
Whispering tales of the night.

Each fluttering wing is a symphony,
A delicate dance of light,
Illuminating the night sky,
With their ethereal grace.

BEAUTY

In the eye of the beholder,
Lies the true beauty.
Not in physical guise,
But in character, sweet and fruity.

Nature's beauty captivates,
Yet human beauty is deeper.
It's not in looks, but in traits,
That we find a soul's keeper.

Deception in attractiveness,
Fades with passing time.
But a person's kindness,
Stays Forever in its prime.

Judge not by appearance,
For it's just a shell.
True beauty is in resilience,
In the heart, it dwells.

Like a jack-fruit's rough exterior,
Hides a sweet surprise,
Beauty is not superior,
It's in what's behind the eyes.

So, let's look beyond the skin,
And see the beauty within,
For in the eye of the beholder,
True beauty will always win.

A DECADENT DELICACY

In the realm of decadent desserts,
There lies a cake that truly asserts,
Its dominance and its rich allure,
Dark chocolate cake, so sweet and pure.

With layers of moist, velvety crumb,
And frosting that could make you numb,
This dessert is a true delight,
A sinful indulgence for the night.

The cocoa powder, so dark and deep,
Infuses the cake with a flavour so sweet,
It melts on your tongue, like a lover's kiss,
Bringing you pure, unadulterated bliss.

The bittersweet taste, a perfect blend,
Balancing scrumptious flavours that never end,
A symphony of chocolate, so pure and rich,
That leaves you longing for just one more stitch.

Each bite is a journey, a sensual ride,
Through layers of cake, so tall and wide,
With creamy frosting, so smooth and divine,
That you swear you could eat it all the time.

Dark chocolate cake, a dessert so grand,
It's like heaven settled on a plate,
As we indulge in its enthralling richness, its pure delight,
And savour every moment, every luring bite.

So next time you crave something sweet,
Reach for a slice of this delectable treat,
Let the dark chocolate cake work its magic on you,
And you'll thank the dessert gods for creating something so true.

In conclusion, dark chocolate cake,
Is a culinary masterpiece that doesn't fake,
Its deliciousness and its pure allure,
Make it a dessert that will always endure.

AROUND THE WORLD

I set off on a journey grand,
To travel the world, across the land.
Through mountains high and oceans deep,
The wonders of the world sure to keep.

I started in a small cafe,
With a map in hand, I found my way.
To distant lands and far-off shores,
Exploring realms unknown before.

I sailed on ships and planes so fast,
Through clouds and stars, a traveller vast.
I danced with locals in the square,
And breathed in scents of foreign air.

I tasted foods I'd never tried,
And learned to speak with tongues that hide.
I climbed the pyramids so tall,
And wandered through ancient walls.

I met with kings and paupers alike,
And shared in joy and sorrow's strike.
I sang with birds in forests green,
And marvelled at sights unseen.

I trekked through jungles, thick and wild,
And crossed deserts, a dusty child.
I swam in seas of azure blue,
And hiked up mountains, a lofty view.

I travelled far and travelled wide,
With an open heart and eyes so wide.
For in the end I have found,
That the world truly is round.

And though our differences are vast,
We share dreams that will forever last.
So let us journey hand in hand,
And travel the world, across the land.

CLICHES

In a world filled with cliches, we dance,
To the rhythm of tired phrases, worn-out words,
Repeating like echoes in the vast expanse of our minds.

We chase after rainbows and search for silver linings,
But find only well-worn paths and tired cliches,
Painted in shades of familiarity and comfort.

We seek solace in the familiar, in the expected,
But lose ourselves in the mundane, the ordinary,
Caught in a web of cliches, we long for something new.

Clichés, those worn-out words and phrases
Threadbare and tired, yet they linger
Echoing through time, recycled and reused.

Like a broken record, they play on,
Filling the air with their monotony,
Lost in the sea of familiarity.
But beneath the surface of clichés,
Lie whispers of truth and wisdom,
Old adages that stand the test of time.

In the midst of the mundane and expected
There can be beauty in the cliché, A comfort in the well-worn path.

So let us embrace the clichés,
And find solace in their familiarity,
For sometimes, in the cliché, we find home.

As we continue to embrace the cliches, the well-worn words.
Finding beauty in the simplicity, in the familiarity,
And finding ourselves reflected in their worn-out lines.

DRENCHING IN THE RAIN

Drenching in the rain, a symphony of nature's tears,
Each drop a whispered secret, each splash a gentle reminder,
Of the power of the sky, of the beauty in the storm.

I stand beneath the heavy clouds, arms outstretched,
Letting the rain wash over me, soaking me to the bone,

Becoming one with the rhythm of the falling drops.

The world around me fades away, blurred by the rain,
Leaves glisten with moisture, earthy scents rise,
A dance of water and light, a canvas of liquid dreams.

In this moment of surrender, I am cleansed,
My worries washed away in the downpour,
I am reborn, renewed, drenched in the rain's embrace.

And as the storm passes, the sun breaks through,
A rainbow arcing across the sky, a promise of hope,
I am left standing, drenched in the rain, but filled with an everlasting light.

SHADOWS

In the quiet corners of the day, shadows dance,,
Stretching long and lean across the earth
They play and twist, shifting with the sun's
gentle arc,
Whispering secrets in the language of dusk.

Dark and mysterious, they cloak the world,
A veil of mystery, a shroud of secrets,
They follow us, mirror our movements,
Always one step behind, one breath away.

In the depths of the night, shadows grow,
Swelling and swelling like a tide,
They engulf the world in their inky embrace,
A cloak of darkness, a blanket of night.

But do not fear the shadows, for they are but friends,
Guiding us through the labyrinth of life,
Showing us the beauty in the darkness,
And the light that shines within.

So let the shadows dance, let them play,
For they are the silent companions of our souls,
Leading us ever closer to the light,
And the truth that lies within.

THE MORNING DEW

In the hush of dawn's embrace,
Glistening jewels adorn the earth,
Morning dew, a delicate grace,
A whispered promise of rebirth.

Each droplet a tiny world,
Reflecting the first light of day,
A shimmering tapestry unfurled,
In the quiet before the fray.

Softly kissed by the sun's gentle touch,
The dew begins to slowly fade,
A fleeting moment, oh so much,
A reminder that beauty doesn't immortally stay.

But in its brief existence,
The morning dew reveals a truth,
That even in the midst of distance,
We can find beauty in our youth.

So let us cherish each new day,
Embrace the magic in the morn,
For in the morning dew's display,
We find hope in being reborn.

BARBIE- PART ONE

There once was a girl with a whim,
For a doll, she had a great trim,
With long golden hair,
And dresses so fair,
Her collection filled to the brim!

The girl was named Barbie,
She lived in a world so far from grubby,
With beauty so rare,
Long silky hair,
Her life was anything but drabby!

In her dream house she'd prance and sway,
In fancy gowns, she'd spend her day,
With Ken by her side,
In love, they'd abide,
In a world where everything's okay.

Barbie dolls, oh what a craze!
Little girls in a Barbie daze,
With outfits galore,
And accessories more,
Their creativity ablaze.

From Malibu to Paris they'd travel,
In convertibles sleek and gravel,
Fashion Week in Milan,
All part of her plan,
To show the world she can unravel.

But beneath the plastic facade,
Lies a message that could seem odd,
For young girls to see,
A perfect Barbie-
Could lead to a flawed spree.

With proportions unrealistic,
Some find Barbie quite simplistic,
Her waist so teeny,
Her legs so lean-y,
Could this ideal be a vamp(stick)?

But Barbie is more than just looks,
She's a symbol for girls in their books,
She's a doctor, a pilot,
A chef and a scientist,
A reminder to follow their hooks.

Let's not judge Barbie way too harsh,
For she's more than just clothes and starch.

She's a role model for girls,
In a world full of swirls,
A constant reminder to reach for the stars.

BARBIE- PART TWO

In a toy store, there sits a Barbie so fair,
With golden locks and clothes beyond compare,
But her plastic smile hides,
The emptiness inside,
Oh, how she longs for love and tender care.

In her dream house, she reigns as a queen,
With a closet full of outfits pristine,
But in the silence of night,
She feels a deep plight,
For she's just a doll, not a living being.

Ken, her handsome partner, stands by her side,
But their love is just a plastic facade, worldwide,
They dance and they twirl,

In their perfect doll world,
But their hearts ache for something real, deep inside.

Little girls play with Barbies each day,
Imagining the adventures they portray,
But behind the painted face,
Lies a hidden grace,
A longing for true love that won't fade away.

So, remember, as you play with your doll,
She may be just plastic, but she has a soul,
In her eyes, there's a spark,
A desire to embark,
On a journey to find love, to be whole.

BUNDLE OF JOY

In the vast expanse of my heart, he resides,
My baby boy, a bundle of joy and light,
A precious gift that fills my days with love,
With every coo and giggle, my soul takes flight.

His eyes, like oceans of wonder and delight,
Reflecting the world in pure innocence,
His tiny hands reach out to touch my face,
And in that moment, time holds no sense.

I watch him grow, a miracle unfolding,
Each milestone a victory, each smile a treasure,
His laughter echoes through the walls of my heart,
A symphony of love that knows no measure.

I watch him sleep, so peaceful and serene,
My sweet baby boy, my heart's saccharine dream,
Each breath he takes, each beat of his heart,
Fills me with love, never to depart.

In his presence, I am whole and complete,
A mother blessed beyond words can convey,
My baby boy, my reason to believe,
In the beauty of life, in love that will never stray.
I'll hold him close, through every tear,
I'll soothe his unnerving fears,
So grow up strong, my little one,
With kindness, love, and an infectious laughter spun,
Know that you are loved beyond measure,
My baby boy, mumma’s greatest treasure.

AROMA OF COFFEE

In the early morning haze, a comforting aroma lingers,
The earthy scent of coffee beans swirling, enveloping my senses,
Rich and bold, like a warm embrace from within,
A symphony of flavors dancing in the air, inviting me in.

The aroma of coffee, a morning delight,
Wakes the senses, stirs the soul from its plight.
The essence of fragrance, rich and bold,
A scent that whispers, "Awake, my spirit, unfold."

The steam rises lazily, a gentle wisp of awakening,
A promise of energy and vitality, awaiting my savoring,
Each sip a journey through time and space,
A moment of solace, a fleeting embrace.

The smell of coffee, a familiar friend,
Guiding me through the day, from beginning to end,
A ritual of comfort, a ritual of peace,
A simple pleasure that never fails to release.

The smell of coffee, a poetic embrace,
A dance of flavors, a tender, loving grace.
It weaves a tapestry of memories,
Of quiet mornings, and moments of serenity.

As I raise my cup to the morning light,
And breathe in deeply, with all my might,
For in this moment, I am whole and free,
In the sacred embrace of the smell of coffee.

INSANELY SANE

In the realm of the wildly sane,
Where chaos dances with reason,
I reside, a paradox incarnate,
An enigma of contradictions.

I am the storm and the calm,
The darkness and the light,
A symphony of contradictions,
A kaleidoscope of thoughts.

My mind is a labyrinth,
A maze of intricate patterns,

A dance of madness and clarity,
A paradoxical masterpiece.

In the realm of the insanely sane,
I find my true reflection,
A mirror of contradictions,
A portrait of complexity.

I embrace the chaos within,
And find peace in the storm,
For in the realm of the wildly sane,
I am truly free to be me.

HOT MESS

Hot mess, a chaotic symphony of disarray,
A swirling tempest of tangled emotions,
A wild dance of tangled hair and rumpled clothes,
A messy collage of scattered thoughts and scattered dreams.

In this messy world, we find beauty in the chaos,
In the imperfection and the raw authenticity,
In the wild and untamed spirit that refuses to be contained,

In the freedom of letting go and embracing the
mess.

Hot mess, a canvas of vibrant colors and messy
strokes,
A masterpiece of unfiltered expression,
A celebration of the messy, the imperfect, the
real,
A reminder that life is messy, and that's okay.

Embrace the mess, let it fill you with its energy,
Let it sweep you off your feet and carry you
away,
Let it be a reminder that perfection is overrated,
And that sometimes, it's the mess that makes us
truly alive.

LULLABY

In the hush of night, the world falls still,
A lullaby whispers on the breeze,
Soft and sweet, a gentle melody,
Guiding weary souls to peaceful dreams.

The stars above twinkle in the dark expanse,
Their light a blanket of comfort and calm,
As the moon watches over with a tender gaze,
Casting a silvery glow upon the land.

In this quiet moment, all is at peace,
The worries of the day drift away,
And in the cradle of the night's embrace,
We find solace in the lullaby's sway.

So close your eyes and let the music soothe,
Let it carry you to a realm of rest,
Where troubles fade and sorrows dissolve,
In the gentle embrace of the lullaby's caress.

UNBIASED OPINIONS

In the vast expanse of thought and perception,
Unbiased opinions stand tall and resolute,
A beacon of truth in a world of distortion,
They shine brightly, unclouded by prejudice.

Unfettered by the chains of personal bias,
They soar high, reaching for clarity and understanding,
A breath of fresh air in a realm of noise and chaos,
They speak with a voice that is clear and unwavering.

In a landscape of conflicting views and agendas,
Unbiased opinions stand firm as a mountain,
Their roots deep and strong, anchored in reason,
They remain steadfast, a guiding light in the darkness.

So let us cherish and protect these rare treasures,
For in their honesty lies the key to enlightenment,
In their purity, we find the path to harmony,
Unbiased opinions, a testament to the power of truth.

EARWORMS

In the chambers of my mind, they crawl and twist,
Earworms, insidious melodies that persist.
Uninvited guests that make their home in my brain,
Echoing tunes that drive me slightly insane.

They slither through my thoughts, a constant hum,
A chorus of voices that never succumb,
Invisible threads weaving through my days,
Playing on repeat in a never-ending maze.

I try to shake them off, to break free,
But they cling to me like a melody.
Whispers of songs that refuse to depart,
A symphony of chaos in my heart.

So I surrender to the earworms' relentless call,
Embracing the music that entwines us all.
For in their haunting, there lies a strange beauty,
A reminder of the power of sound's duty.

And so I let them sing, let them dance and play,
For in their melody, I find my own way.
Earworms, a strange gift that never fades,
A symphony of life in the melodies they parade.

GUSHING WAVES

Majestic and powerful,
The gushing waves crash,
Against the shore,
A symphony of nature's might.

Upon the shore, they come to play,
Gushing waves, in a rhythmic sway.
Their whispers soft, their roars loud,
A dance of nature, loud and proud.

Rising high and falling low,
Their rhythm never falters,
A dance of chaos and calm,
Infinite and eternal.

In hues of blue and white they frolic,
Their tales of mystery, they unravel,
A symphony of life, they compose,
In the heart of the ocean, they roam.

Their touch, a gentle caress,
A soothing lullaby, they address,
To the sands, they whisper secrets,
In the language of the tides, they beckon.

Each crest a masterpiece,
Each trough a mystery,
They move with purpose,
Unstoppable and untamed.

The ocean's heartbeat,
A pulse of life and energy,
Endless and vast,
A force of nature's beauty.

Gushing waves, relentless,
Carving their path,
Leaving a trail of wonder,
In their wake.

Oh, gushing waves, your beauty unveiled,
A masterpiece of nature, wild and beguiled,
In your rhythm, we find our voice,
In your embrace, we find solace.

SHOOTING STARS

Oh, the night sky, a canvas of wonder,
A tapestry of twinkling lights, a true thunder,
The shooting stars, they dance and play,
A celestial show, in a cosmic sway.

Their trails of light, like glowing brushes,
Paint the sky with colors of the rushes,
A palette of hues, a symphony of light,
A celestial ballet, a wondrous sight.

The stars, they twinkle and sparkle with glee,
As they streak across the velvet sea,
Their paths, a mystery, a wonder to see,
A cosmic dance, for all humanity.

Oh, the magic of the night sky,

A treasure trove of wonder and sigh,
The shooting stars, a cosmic delight,
A celestial show, a true wonder in sight.

BUBBLES

Bubbles rise like dreams in the morning light,
Glistening orbs of shimmering delight,
Drifting, dancing, floating high,
Reflecting rainbows in the sky.

Their translucent skins, a glistening glow,
Refracting sunbeams, as they flow.
In the breeze, they swirl and twirl,
A delicate ballet, beyond compare.

They're delicate and fleeting, yet so strong,
A transient beauty that won't be long,
Sparkling in the sun's warm embrace,
A moment of magic, a fleeting grace.

Each bubble holds a world within,
A tiny universe, a joyful spin,
A reminder of the simple things,
That makes our hearts flutter and sing.

So let's embrace the bubbles, large and bright,
Let them lift our spirits, take us to new heights,
For in their fragile beauty, we find,
A sense of wonder, pure and kind.

TEARDROPS

Teardrops cascade like gentle rain,
Each one a story untold, a pain unspoken.
They fall silently, a whisper of sorrow,
Leaving a trail of emotions in their wake.

In the quiet of night, they shimmer and gleam,
Reflecting the moon's soft glow,
A mirror to the soul's deepest yearnings,
A release of the heart's hidden depths.

Each teardrop holds a universe within,
A universe of memories, of hopes, of fears.
They speak of love lost, of dreams shattered,
Of moments of pure joy and profound sadness.

And as they fall, one by one,
They water the garden of the soul,
Nourishing the seeds of resilience and strength,
And allowing the beauty of healing to grow.

So let the teardrops flow freely,
For they are the essence of our humanity,
A testament to our capacity to feel,
To love, to hurt, to heal, to be.

And in their shimmering beauty,
We find solace in the knowledge,
That even in our darkest moments,
Teardrops can be a source of light and renewal.

MY FAVOURITE SONG

In the silence of the night, I find solace,
In the melody that echoes in my soul,
A favorite song that speaks to my heart,
A symphony of emotions, a work of art.

Each note a whisper of memories past,
Each chord a reminder that nothing lasts,
But in this moment, time stands still,
As the music weaves its magical thrill.

The lyrics dance like poetry in the air,
A story of love, of joy, of despair,
A song that resonates deep within.
A connection that's pure, a beautiful sin.

I close my eyes and let the music take flight,
Guiding me through the darkness of the night,
My favorite song, my guiding light,
A companion that's always by my side.

So I'll cherish these moments, hold them dear,
For the song that I love will always be near,
A melody that soothes, a rhythm that moves,
My favorite song, my heart approves.

DEFYING AGES

Orange orchid, just a kid,
Under the shade, he slid, he hid,
Black void, who seems annoyed,
Feelings toyed, two broken boys.

Of each other, they were not fond,
“You’re too empty!” cried the tangerine blond,
“And you’re too full,” the other did respond.

Alas, even puzzle pieces that don’t seem to fit,
Once turned around, it seemed to click.
Loneliness made the void lovesick,
Heartbreak made the stars ache.
With thorns, the orchids were surrounded,

They burn, and to ashes, they turn.
"You're out of my reach," said the orchid,
"I am nothing but a speck in your eyes."

To this, the void responded, with a gentle smile,
With eyes of jade, laid upon his lover,
"I may be the sky, but I need you,
Like the truth needs a lie,
Like grief needs to cry.
Even I, as the void, am overjoyed,
To be spoiled by your admiration.
We are together, from one dusk to another dawn,
Time after time, our references shall be drawn.
Our union shall be seen like orion,
Each time we meet at the horizon."

In a world of fleeting romances,
Timeless love enhances,
Their bond transcending eras,
Their love defying ages.

Through wars and hardships, they sail,
In joy and pain, they still prevail,
Holding on tight, like a ship in a gale,
Their love, an eternal tale.

A beacon in the darkest nights,
Binding them in passionate lights,
Time may pass, but their love takes flight,

Two souls entwined, burning bright.
In a world of constant change,
They remain, beautifully strange,
An unbreakable force, never estranged,
Forever and always, as fate arranged.

STRAY DOG

In the heart of the city, a stray dog roams,
Through alleyways and streets, a place that it calls home,
With fur matted and eyes filled with sorrow,
Seeking scraps of food, a hopeful tomorrow.

Lost and forgotten, yet resilient and strong,
Surviving each day, where it doesn't belong,
A creature of instinct, a fighter at best,
Enduring the hardships, passing each test.

In the shadows it lurks, a ghost in the night,
A silent companion, seeking solace in its flight,
No collar, no tag, just the wind in its fur,
A lone wanderer, guided by a distant star.

Scavenging for scraps, a feast in the trash,
A survivor of neglect, a life lived in flash,
Through rain and through sunshine, it
perseveres,
A symbol of freedom, conquering fears.

So let us not judge, but show kindness instead,
For in the eyes of a stray dog, lies a story unsaid,
Of resilience and courage, of survival and grace,
A reminder to cherish each moment we face.

THE TEA STALL

In a bustling market square, where vendors all abound,
A humble tea stall stood, with a warm and cozy sound.
The scent of brewed tea and sweet pastries filled the air,
Inviting all to stop and linger, without a care.

Patrons gather around, a diverse tapestry of faces,
Each with their own stories and dreams,
Bound together by a shared love for this humble brew.

Conversations flow like the tea itself,
Laughter, debates, and delicate confessions,
Echoing through the makeshift walls of the stall.

The stall was run by a kind old man, with a twinkle in his eye,
Who poured the tea with skill and grace, never shy.
He'd chat with customers, and share stories of his youth,
As they sipped their tea, and savored the sweet truth.
The tea was a blend of the finest leaves, with a hint of spice,
That warmed the heart and soothed the soul, so nice.
The cups were delicate, with intricate designs,
That added to the charm, and made the moment shine.

The pastries were freshly baked, with a golden crust,
That melted in the mouth, and left a lasting trust.
From scones to tarts, and cakes to pies,
There was something for everyone, to satisfy.

The tea stall was a haven, a place to rest,
From the hustle and bustle, and the daily test.
A place to connect, and share a smile,
In the heart of the market, for a little while.

So if you're in the area, do stop by,
And taste the magic of this tea stall nearby.
A moment of peace, and a cup of cheer,
You'll find it here, without a speck of fear.

CHEESE BURST PIZZA

Oh, the cheese burst pizza, a culinary delight,
A flavorful feast for the taste buds, an enticing ignite,
With melted cheese and savory sauce, it's a treat to bite,
A masterpiece of flavors, a true gastronomic sight.

A cheese burst masterpiece, a culinary wonder,
Oozing with goodness, a feast to plunder.
Mozzarella and cheddar in a harmonious dance,
Stretching and melting in a cheesy romance.
A golden crust, a canvas for the cheese to burst,
Each bite an orchestration, a culinary thirst.

The crust, so crispy and golden, a perfect base,
Topped with mounds of cheese, it's a joy to embrace,

The sauce, a tangy blend of herbs and spices,
supremely fine.
Adds depth and richness to each and every bite,
paramountly divine.

The toppings, a symphony of flavors and
textures far from bland,
Pepperoni, sausage, mushrooms, and onions, ah,
all so grand!
The cheese, a velvety blanket of melted delight,
A culinary masterpiece, a true work of art,
fiercely bright.

Oh, the cheese burst pizza, a true gastronomic
dream,
A ravishing journey that will leave you beaming,
So take a bite, and let the magic unfold,
A delicious adventure that will leave you
wanting more.

Indulge in the gooey goodness, savor each bite,
In the world of pizza, this one takes a flight.
A cheese lover's dream, a gastronomic delight,
The cheese burst pizza, a true culinary sight.

BROKEN PROMISES

Broken promises, like shattered dreams,
Leave us with scars that rarely heal,
A heavy heart and tears unseen,
A future once bright, now bleak and lean.

Memories of what could have been,
Haunt us like a ghostly presence,
The pain of loss and heartache keen,
A burden we can't dismiss.

The weight of broken trust,
A burden we can't shake,
Like a shadow that won't depart,
A lingering hurt that won't break.

The words that were said with ease,
Now ring an echoing hollow in our ears,
The lies that were told with grace,
Leave us with wounds that won't readily cease.

The dreams we had, now shattered and gone,
Leave us with an everlasting hollow feeling,
The love we thought was true,
Is now nothing but a fleeting thrill.

FAMILIAR FRAGRANCES

In the gardens of delight, where flowers bloom and sway,
A familiar fragrance fills the air, each day.
It's the scent of memories, of joy and grace,
A perfume that lingers, a wondrous embrace.

The sweetness of rose petals, delicate and fine,
Mingles with the spice of lavender's design.
The heady aroma of jasmine, so pure and light,
Dances on the breeze, a wondrous sight.

The fragrance of home, where love resides,
Where laughter and tears, and memories abide.
A comforting scent, that never fades away,
A familiar fragrance that brightens each day.

The gentle whispers of lilac's sigh,
The subtle hint of sandalwood, so high.
The warm embrace of vanilla's sweet delight,
A symphony of scents, a true delight.

In every place, where love resides,
A familiar fragrance that never hides.
A memory of joy, a feeling so true,
A scent that lingers, a heart that's anew.

COMMON SENSE

In a world of reality far away from dreams,
Where common sense is not what it seems,
A rich kid and his friend converse,
About a story, for better or worse.

In a tale of riches and tears,
A poor man's fate appears,
With a magic cup in hand,
His sorrow turned to pearls so grand.

On a mountain of wealth he sat,
With a knife stained, his heart grew flat,
His wife now lifeless in his embrace,
A gruesome end to riches' chase.

The friend, with a question wise,
Asked of the man's dark demise,
"Why take a life to shed a tear,
When an alternative could have brought you near?"
"Why not just cut an onion, to cry?
Instead of making someone deliberately die?

Common sense is a rare gift indeed!

HARD WORK VS SMART WORK

In the kingdom of old, a king did reside,
Three sons he had, his realm to decide.
To find the heir, a task was set,
To fill a room without a gap, a challenge to be met.

The first son chose stones, big and grand,
But gaps remained, not what he planned.
The second son chose hay to lay,
Yet gaps still lingered, despite the display.

The third son thought, with wisdom in mind,
To his dressing room, a solution to find.
A bottle of liquid, a fragrance so rare,
He sprinkled it gently, filling the air.
Jasmine's aroma, sweet and pure,
Filled the room, a scent to endure.
No gaps were found, no space to spare,
The king knew his heir, with certainty rare.

In the pursuit of success, we are told,
To work hard and be bold.
But the true secret, I'm here to say,
A smart plan and a bit of hard work paves the way.

Better is to combine the two,
Hard work with a smart view.
With goals in sight and success as the aim,
Work hard and smartly rise to fame.

RISE FROM THE ASHES

Deep within the depths of despair, where darkness reigns,
A flicker of hope, a spark remains.
From the ruins of devastation and pain,
A phoenix emerges, rising again.

Through the flames of adversity, it soars,
Defying the odds, opening new doors.
With wings of strength and a heart ablaze,
It spreads its wings in a fiery blaze.

From the ashes of what once was lost,
A new beginning, a higher cost.
The phoenix rises, bold and strong,
A symbol of resilience all along.

So let us learn from this majestic bird,
To rise from the ashes, undeterred.
To embrace the flames that once consumed,
And emerge victorious and unperturbed.

For in the fire, we find our power,
To rise above, to bloom and flower.
To transform our pain into our light,
And shine as brightly as the night.

So let us be like the phoenix-mighty and wise,
And rise from the ashes, to touch the skies.
To embrace our scars, our flaws, our fears,
And emerge stronger through our tears.

SATIRE

In satire's realm, where wit doth reign,
A world of mockery, a world of pain.
Where hypocrisy and folly displayed,
And pride and prejudice are here to stay.

The satirist's pen doth wield great power,
To pierce the mask every hour.
With biting words, they cut so deep,
And lay bare the foolishness we keep.

In satire's eye, all is a game,
Where vice and virtue are but a claim.
Their sharp words doth slice through the air,
And leave us all in a state of despair.

But oh, the beauty of their art,
Their words doth dance upon the heart.
For though they mock and they deride,
They show us truths we cannot hide.

So let us embrace satire's grace,
And heed the lessons of its place.
For in its mocking, we may see,
The truths that we so desperately need.

FALLEN ANGEL

In the shadows of the night, a fallen angel wanders,
Her wings once radiant and pure, now tattered and torn,
Cast out from the heavens, she roams the earthly realm,
A solitary figure, haunted by her past.

Her eyes hold the weight of centuries,
Glimmering with sorrow and regret,
A soul adrift in a sea of darkness,
Seeking redemption that never comes.

She walks among mortals, unseen and unheard,
A ghostly presence in a world that has forgotten her,
Her beauty faded, her grace diminished,
A once celestial being now lost and alone.

But beneath the surface of her pain,
There lies a spark of hope,
A flicker of light in the endless night,
A reminder of the angel she once was.

And though she may be fallen,
She still carries within her the essence of divinity,
A testament to the power of forgiveness,
A symbol of grace in a world of chaos.

So let us not judge her for her transgressions,
But instead, let us offer her our compassion,

For even fallen angels deserve a chance at redemption,
A chance to rise once more and soar among the stars.

COMEDY

Comedy dances with wild abandon,
A tapestry woven with wit and whimsy,
Unfurling in the theater of the absurd.

It is the jester's jest,
The clown's caper,
The comic's clever quip,
A symphony of smiles and chuckles.

From slapstick to satire,
From puns to parodies,
Comedy wears many masks,
Each one way more hilarious than the last.

Comedy clubs and open mics,
Amateur comedians take their strikes,
The thrill of making a room burst with laughter,
A feeling like no other, pure rapture.

Tickling our funny bone at the helm,
From sitcoms to rom-coms, dark humor and more,
Laughter is what we all adore.
From slapstick to satire, wit and charm,
Funny bones tickled, spirits made warm,

Improv comedy, witty banter,
Quick thinking, fast retort, the banter.

Thinking on your feet, comedy gold,
Audiences left in stitches, stories retold.

It is the antidote to sorrow,
The balm for every weary soul,
A reminder that even in darkness,
There is room for joy and mirth.

So let us revel in the absurd,
Embrace the unexpected twist,
For in the world of comedy,
There is room for all to laugh and exist.

SELFIES

In the days of old, before the digital craze,
When photos were simple, without much haze,
A smile was dragged across each face,
A "V-sign" for the teens, a jaunty grace.

No hand on hip, no perfect pose,
Just keeping eyes open, not holding the phone.
A facetious "ta-da!" or a kissy face,
No filters or tricks, just natural grace.

But now, in the age of social media's reign,
We strike a pose, trying to attain,
Perfection in every selfie shot we take,
Emulating the stars, for our own sake.

Scrolling through timelines, it's hard to ignore,
The pouts, the poses, the quest for flawless
selfies ever more.
But in those simple days of old,
True beauty shone, unfiltered and bold.

EMPATHY

On a Sunday morning, calm and serene,

The NYC subway, a peaceful scene.

Passengers reading, some in a doze,

Through the city's depths, the train flows.

A station arrives, a man with kids in tow,

Board the train, their energy aglow.

Chaos erupts, the calm is shattered,

Children running wild, noise scattered.

The once quiet ride, now full of sound,

Kids shouting, screaming, wrestling around.

The subway car, a lively stage,

With children's laughter, filling the page.

The father stood still, silent, unmoved,

As chaos erupted, children's voices grooved.

Passengers shifted, unease in their eyes,

Anger and frustration, a collective sigh.

No attempt made, no intervention seen,

Just a father watching, calm, serene.

Elderly passengers disturbed from sleep,

Their thoughts filled with annoyance deep.

"Why won't he quiet them down?"

"Such poorly raised kids, a frown."

Horrible, annoying, the whispers spread,

As they wished for peace instead.

The father's inaction, a mystery unsolved,

In every mind, the same question revolved.

A word, a command, a parental stance,

But silence prevailed, no action, no chance.

A poem of a father's quiet demeanor,

While chaos reigned, a silent screamer.

Unmoving, untouched by the unrest,

A father's presence put to test.

In a crowded train carriage,

Amidst the hustle and bustle,

A well-dressed man in a bowler hat,

Could no longer contain his tussle.

He approached a father with kids,

Grabbed his collar, shouted in rage,

"Put them in order, do something now!"

His anger on an escalating stage.

The father looked up, eyes filled with sorrow,

Spoke slowly, words heavy with grief,

"We just came back from the hospital,

Their mother passed, it's beyond belief."

Tears welled up in his tired eyes,

Streaming down his weathered face,

The businessman's grip slowly released,

Apologizing, leaving his place.

The carriage's mood took a turn,

From anger to empathy's embrace,

A lesson learned in a moment's span,

Of compassion and understanding's grace.

If we could read the secret history,

Of our enemies, a mystery untold,

In each man's life, a tale of sorrow,

Enough to soften hearts grown cold.

Suffering and pain, a common thread,

Binding us in shared humanity,

Disarm all hostility, instead,

With unquestionable empathy.

TODDLERS

Where little feet patter and laughter rings,
A world of discovery, untamed and wild,
Toddlers roam, fearless and free.

Their spirits untamed, their hearts pure,
Curiosity sparkles in their eyes,
Each moment a new adventure,
Each discovery is a triumph to celebrate.

In their tiny hands, the world is a canvas,
Painted with joy, mischief, and love,
Their laughter echoes like a melody,
Their innocence- a beacon in the darkness

Oh, toddlers of boundless energy,
You are the poets of the everyday,

With your clumsy steps and sweet babbles,
You remind us of the beauty in simplicity.

May you never lose your sense of wonder,
May you always dance with joy in your heart,
For in your presence, we find solace,
In the magic of your pure, untamed spirit.

GOODBYES

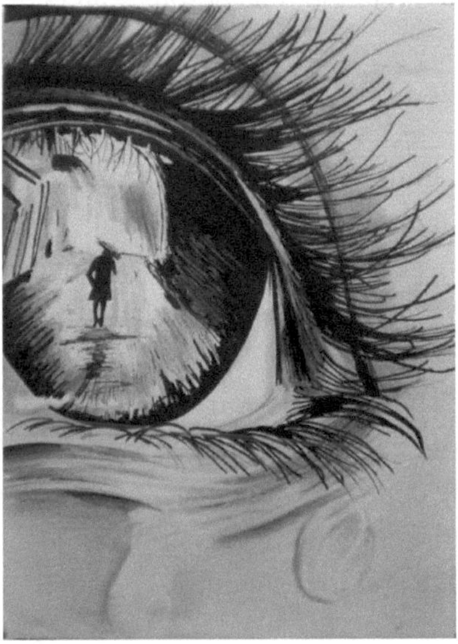

In the hushed moments between heartbeats,
We find ourselves standing at the edge of a farewell,
Where time hangs heavy like an anchor,
And words lose their meaning in the weight of emotion.

Goodbyes linger in the air like a bitter taste,
A bitter symphony of memories and regrets,
Echoing through the chambers of our souls,
Leaving us breathless and broken.

The silence stretches out like a vast ocean,
Unforgiving and cold,
As we navigate the treacherous waters of parting,
Struggling to find solid ground beneath our feet.

And yet, in the midst of this storm,
There is a quiet beauty to be found,
A bittersweet melody that sings of love,
Of the precious moments we shared together.

So let us embrace this sorrow,
Let us hold each other close,
For in the depths of goodbye,
We find the strength to carry on,
And to live and love again.

9 789360 94408

Printed by Libri Plureos GmbH in Hamburg, Germany